IN
SEARCH
OF

Healing Through
Mental Health Poetry

Jordan
Brown

IN SEARCH OF HAPPINESS

© 2020 Jordan Brown

Cover design: Lindsay Armistead

Interior design: Ljiljana Pavkov

To my wife, Kristie

Without you, there would be no poetry

And to my parents

For teaching me to write and to coach,

and to know how to put my heart equally into both

Table of Contents

ANXIETY

SOCIETY

HEALING

MEANING

IN
SEARCH
OF
happiness

ANXIETY

Anxiety Is

anxiety is a fickle foe
the webs it weaves
the wind it blows
the empty air, who even knows
the fickle foe, anxiety

anxiety is an open sore
the more exposed
the more it roars
with nagging aches, forevermore
the open sore, anxiety

anxiety is a breathless dream
of restless nights
and bursting seams
spotlight on, sweat that gleams
the breathless dream, anxiety

Body of Anxiety

Let's take it from the top
The head, the throbbing head
Filled with wires,
Snapping and flailing
Chancing connection
Through misfiring neurons
That reach the neck
Taut with unnoticed tension
Glued to the head
And to the back
In one immovable block
Arms, the floating arms
Detached at times
Or tethered too tight
In their fight
To escape the body
But their fidgets belie
Their purpose
To squeeze, to hold, to grab
On to something firm
A counterweight, a countermeasure
From steadier times
Days when the legs moved
In much the same way
And covered distances
Effortless, breathless distances
Still, to this day they move

Trudging forward
One by one, the same way
Whether trouncing ruins
Of old dreams
Or delicate shards
Of future remnants
Which are pointy objects
That pierce the feet
And prick the skin
Sending shockwaves
Back to the head

The Feeling of "Not Good Enough"

I **HATE** that I feel this way.

It's a feeling that I try hard to shake — the feeling of "not good enough."

Take the word "good" in that last line, and it could easily be "brave" or "strong" or "smart."

I don't feel good enough most of the time.

I don't think I could explain it to you, although I'm going to try.

First, I need to ask, "Good enough for whom?"

I think I'll just evade the question and look for a new one.

THAT question makes me put my head down.

It leaves me with an answer that's safer if it's locked away where no one can see it.

The answer is: "good enough for me," of course.

It's the answer I shy away from because I don't want to admit that I know it, that I'm plagued by it.

If I tell you it's to be good enough for my friends, or my family, or that stranger I helped on the street — well, that would be a lie.

But attaching my worth to what others say is easier. It's safer.

Generating my own idea of self-worth is terrifying and fraught with consequences.

If I have to create the measure which I meet or fall short of, then only I am to blame.

So I shove it off on others.

I take what they tell me, and I measure myself against **THEIR** standards.

It doesn't matter if I agree with them or not. It doesn't matter if it's not close to identifying who I really am. It doesn't matter.

And when nothing matters, anything goes.

I tried something new the other day.

It's based on positive thinking. It's something I thought couldn't be **NEARLY** as effective as anxiously planning every single detail of my life.

The first twenty-five years of my life were meticulously planned for.

I achieved some things, but I wasn't **LIVING**. The tension in my neck and shoulders never went away. The negative self-talk etched jagged lines down my back.

I never told myself I wanted to be a drill sergeant, but I had spent my whole life training to be one.

Until, one day, I tried saying nice things to myself.

WHAT A JOKE, I thought.

And there I went again — my first thought, a negative one.

Then I took a deep breath.

I looked in the mirror — the same one where I have spent countless ruminating hours — and said, "You are confident. You are capable. You are likable."

I was the one-man star in my own tragic comedy.

That idea made me smile, it created some light.

And I carried that little spark of an idea with me throughout the day.
Instead of planning my day, I said nice things to myself.
Instead of fixating on the past, I said nice things to myself.
It made me smile to think how ridiculous I must look.
But then I noticed someone was smiling at me as she walked by. That made me smile even more.
My thoughts had tricked me into acting in a way I hadn't predicted. **THAT** changed my actions, which **THEN** changed my environment.

How could something so simple be so amazing?

A simple reminder to say nice things to myself.
It's what parents teach their children but forget to teach themselves.
And the kids grow up to be there for others but torment the face in the mirror.
It's not so preposterous when you think about how it happens.
As a result, to measure if I was "good enough," I learned to use others as my reference point.
I had no point of reference for who **I WAS** as a person.
And now that I have one, I can only compare who I am to **MYSELF**.
That means one of us has to be "good" if the other's not "good enough."

My Time As a Child, Thinking of Today

I remember, when I was a boy
Thinking things would get easier
That adults knew
What to do
How to act
And what to be
All it takes is time
I thought
All it takes is time

Now I know
That grown-ups
Have the same thoughts
But also have the same feelings
Of fear
Of anxiety
Of loneliness
That children have
They may
Even have more
Feelings
Like regret and grief
Despair and dread
A child has grown-up worries
A grown-up has childlike fear

A child who learns to outrun

His feelings

Becomes an adult

Whose feelings

Catch him

There's no outrunning

Something that bursts

From within

Without them

Life is a bore

With them

Life is finding a way

To swim upstream

But only as far

As it takes to learn

That freedom is not in the thrashing

But in the decision

To let go

To let the waves wash over

Like a child feeling the power

Of first-time, well-cried tears

Grab Your Anxiety—and
Let It Go

Grab your anxiety and let it go.
Feel its edges, touch its sides
Know its ridges, trace its lines
Explore its boundaries, as they flow
Grab your anxiety — and let it go.
Shoulder its weights
Filter its fumes
Move past obstacles
And through crowded rooms
Unreal identity
Your self ebbs and flows
Grab your anxiety — and let it go.

Peel back its covers
Untell the lies
Retract the visions
And selfish disguise

Follow your heart
Wherever it goes
Grab your anxiety
And then let it go.

In My Head, the Only Place
I Really Know

In my head
Is a dreamland
It's thought, it's hope, it's aspiration
It's a culling of doubt
A carving of the landscape
For more dreams to grow

The thinking fills my head
It creates masterpieces
Scenarios
Of words I will never say
In the way that I think them
Maybe one day
This exact scenario
Will come to pass
But that day
Has not yet arrived
And the question is
Do I want it to?
Or do I want to leave it
In my head
The only place I really know

Anxious and Unafraid

As a child,
Many a night I awoke
With a fast-beating heart
Wrenched from
The dream that seemed
More real
Than the friendly darkness
Of my bedroom

Just a bad dream
I thought
Just a bad dream
Still, I called
For my mother
To tell me what
I already knew

Now I know
Even more
About dreams
They're neither good nor bad
My thinking makes them so
A dream to escape
A nightmare to escape
Change the word and
I change the story

My dreams of anxiety
Where nothing would go right
Aren't just past tense
Still, I dream
Times still I wake
Wrenched from
The vivid lights of neon dreams
Their fast-fading remnants
Lighting a less familiar room
It was just a bad dream
These words I think
To myself

And then
The words
That I keep
To myself
As I awaken further
Into the somnambulance of
Learning to live
Learning to be
Anxious and unafraid

Anxiety, a Familiar Tale

Listen to me now. I'll tell you a tale.

The thoughts in my mind that won't go away. The words whispering between my ears.

There will be times when it's hard to find the silence. There will be days that pass by without realizing where they went.

That's alright. My thoughts don't define me.

Bombardments of thought. My brain is a bellows of airy figments. Remnants of days past. Residue of another time.

It's hard to get the space to stop and properly think when my brain becomes accustomed to its own form of thinking.

That ceaseless process that never stops. The words that keep flowing from my mind.

And my mind just won't turn off. It's not a dishwasher, after all.

It's a living, throbbing thing, even if there are times that I feel it is apart from me, acting separately, living on its own.

I am forever connected to my mind, but that doesn't mean I have to do what it says.

Finding my awareness, focusing on my breath, I can develop space between me and my thoughts

And once I create the space, the world is limitless, and opportunities emerge.

Possibilities that I was missing because the machinery in my head wouldn't break down, although I wanted it to.

What if the point isn't for it to break down, but for it to become well-oiled and controllable, with me as the calm and doting master? What if to conquer the machinery I need to see the machinery for what it is — oily, creaking parts and all?

Can I step outside of my mind and appreciate how the process works?

Anxiety is getting lost in the process. It's not seeing the forest for the trees. It's not even knowing that there are leaves and branches attached to those trees because I'm so caught up in the brambles of my mind.

Does this all sound familiar?

As I get to know the ways in which my mind gets stuck, I come to discover what I need to do to rise above it.

And rise above it I will.

Productivity, success, excellence in what I do — those don't come from stopping the thoughts. Thoughts have a purpose once I learn to direct them.

No, I **NEED** thoughts to decide on the steps I will take, the decisions I will make — all for the sake of creating a life.

Just don't let the thoughts blend into my days. Don't let them become months and years of mental machinations.

Figure out who *I am* beneath my thoughts

Take the time each day to be silent. Learn to be uncomfort-
able so I have a good idea of what comforts me.

I can't do this if I'm thinking.

I know, anxiety often determines whether I think or not.

But I breathe deeply. I ground myself. I'm kind to myself.

There are millions of men and women who have lived life-
times in their heads.

If I ask one of them about their thoughts, I may find the
answer to one of my own.

The Landscape of Doubt

Doubt is a heavy weight
A burden to bear
A winter coat in summer, silly
But suffocating nonetheless
Movement, the antidote
Wherever it takes you
It sheds the second skin
Of doubt
Be curious
But not overly so
Look inward
But don't stay there
Be brave
In staring down roads unseen
Hold out your hands
Don't go it alone
You aren't the first doubt
To walk these paths
Use their footprints
Trace their outlines
To give shape to your fears
And carry your doubt

You Can't Write Poetry
About Depression

You can't write poetry about depression
You have to feel it
It has to seep out of your bones
It has to leak out of your eyes
The poetry is in the becoming
the shifting feeling
the falling breath
the terror of monotony
the naked desperation
the losing of hope
and the long wondering if it will ever return

You can't write poetry about depression
You have to experience it
You have to know it like a brother
And you have to hate it
so much that
you use it
you terrorize it
for what it d`id to you
Until you see the sudden strength
hidden within the darkness
Until you become the darkness
and in so doing
you realize
you've always had the light

The Second Before You Respond
What breaks the whole
subsumes it
What breaks your heart
consumes it
Trying to run from your fate
is like trying to dodge the wind
You're everywhere
and nowhere
all at once

You're chaos veiled with narrative
You're narrative veiled with a smile
Belying the raging rapids, your life
is your personal turmoil
In its churn
you gleefully gasp
tricked by the importance
of your own words
Can you outrun your doubts?
Can you wait for your destiny?
Your answer isn't important
What matters
is the second right before you respond

Digital Compassion

what if we gave
equal attention and care
to the relationships we have
as we do
to the things we buy

                    screen scratched
                        deep sorrow
                    promises broken
                        no big deal

the next big thing
we buy it
the next big act of kindness
for a loved one
appears, on the screen

                            we type it
                            we send it
                            we wish it
                    prayers and thoughts
                        delivered digitally
                the emotions we feel?
                they're not the same

Help Is an Arrogant Act

Help is an arrogant act
An uninvited reaching out
To the other
Who did not invite you there
Who could not invite you there
Because you would not allow it

The helper sees the problems
Sets the bone
And mends the cloth around it
Knowing not the dreams
Of the skin and bones he helps

Help is one-sided
An act of service
A gift given
Without question, without regard
Of the other's inner wishes
Or if he wished for gifts at all

Maybe help is not what is lacking
Maybe it's peace
Assurance
Warmth of body
Keeping company
Listening, feeling
And hoping alongside another
To know what helps

He Who Humiliates

There is nothing so small
as humiliation
Abusing a power imbalance
to crush and silence another
will neither sow new seeds
of progress
nor plow new fields
of success
He who humiliates
is small indeed
and no ounce of weight
pushed down upon
a hapless foe
will change that
Respect
comes from the soil
the tender ground
on which
you and I walk
the same ground
that the tyrant robs
to build fortresses
in a cavernous pit
where no one will ever see him

Call and Response

Do you remember
the time I asked you
if you missed me?
The way
my words fell
like leaden petals
and stayed there,
refusing to die

                          Were you there
                       when I asked you
                             if being alone
                         is different from
                            being lonely?
              Your lack of response
                        carved the air,
           marked with negation

Will you hear the words
I'm about to speak?
Or will they pass through you
on their way back to me
as weary, forgotten echoes

SOCIETY

The Mask

Facing the day
Braving the storm
Wearing the mask
Living the norm
Stilling the urge
Making the climb
Being the best
Playing the mime
Trudging on home
Toeing the line
Taking it off
It's finally time

Daily Grind

Life is a daily grind
The drip, drip of responsibility
Percolating through your bones

The jolt of energy
Followed by the crash
Of overwork

Slurp it up
Or space it out
Until life brews up
The daily grind

Being Busy

How's it going?
Alright. Just busy.
Just busy?
Just busy.
Everyone's busy
doing something these days
Thing is,
I'm not sure what
we're all doing
Are we busy creating art?
Not quite.
The world would have more beauty
If that were the case
Are we busy doing work?
We are.
But what work, exactly?
Is it work that innervates our body?
Or is it work
that props us up
like lifeless mannequins,
storefront puppets on display
If you're in a rush
you can walk by
and they seem real
but they're not
We're too busy to notice
And that's what they count on,
those who sell their wares
to we the masses
who can't pinpoint

what the emptiness
feels like
So we fill the space
with things
that make us busier,
just in different ways
And soon,
the buzzing sound
catches up with us
and it's not
the one
coming from our smartphones
It's the existential dread
clashing
with the deafening clang
of lost meaning

Did you hear what I said?
Were you listening?
What's that?
You're busy?
Never mind.

At Least It's Friday

Millions of people
Hating work
Hoping for something more
Doing what they need to
But not what they want to
Desperate for change
And for sleep
Feeling like actors
In someone else's drama

Putting in time
Taking out money
Shuffling through similar scenes
That blend together
Into a mixture of
offices, walls, people and faces
Meetings of bodies
With minds left at the door,
all thinking the same thought
At least it's Friday

College Campus

on campus
double standards abound
boys wear sweats, with holes
girls wear tights, with sheer
boys wear shoes, with dirt
girls wear heels, with straps
dressed-down masculinity
hyped-up sexuality
seen on campus

girls prepared, yet tense
boys relaxed, yet tense
it's a communal pressure cooker
leaving space to experiment
but everyone is the same

open doorways
lead to image-obsessed minds
attached to image-obsessed phones
inside of image-obsessed colleges
where the customer
is always right

Shame Is a Box

Shame is a box.

Silence, its walls.

Inside, the air is stale. Nothing gets in. Nothing goes out. Just the lingering, rancid stench of shame.

And shame is not an easy feeling to handle.

If it feels oppressive, it's because it **IS** oppressive. Of all the tools in the public's tool belt, shame packs a hefty punch. Social media missives become missiles, targeted to destroy.

Sent to enclose the person in his box, inside of his shame.

The world feels small in there.

But a box is a box, not a castle. It's not an impenetrable fortress.

That's the funny thing about shame.

The walls are made of silence, and they can be walked through at any time. It's the fear of failure, of annihilation, that keeps the person contained within the walls of shame.

But there **IS** a way out.

It starts with truth, and it comes from within. It's a budding awareness that grows and grows until the person in the box outgrows the box — and slides through the walls of shame.

Fortunately, truth knows no bounds. Self-love is shapeless. It's a chameleon.

Because it knows no shape, its potential is unlimited.

That which is formless fits no box.

Needless Death

What will drive us to act
on the needless deaths
from mental health crisis
It's not about personal failure
Not bad character
Not individual flaws
It's collective responsibility
Why does it not devastate us
to read about yet another death
It could be you
It could be me
It *will* be all of us
If we do not act

Systems will save us
so we must create them
New systems
that we imbue with hope
that we stitch with love
that we repair with our own pain
Vibrant
responsive
systems
must be forged by humanity
for humanity
to save us from ourselves

What Does It Take
to Heal a Wound?

What does it take to heal a wound?

to silence a scar?

you cannot suffocate it

you cannot force a door to close

an ending must come

when the path

suddenly ends

when

your hope

tips the scale

and becomes greater

than the weight

in your heart

HEALING

You Are Entropy

When I fall into you
I fall into entropy
And it doesn't bother me
nor does it scare me
Because your entropy
is familiar
and comfortable
Like a favorite sweater
Well worn
Encasing me in known tangles
Covering me in familiar holes
Chaos is only a mindset
but it's a mindset I can handle
A state of being that swallows me
And shoots me out
Into a world of order
Where nothing seems right at all

Holding Your Doors

I want you to know
I hear what you say
See what you mean
I'm with you today

> The road you are on
> Is not mine to walk
> But all roads connect
> The more that we talk

Your life is your life
And mine is my own
But when you feel lonely
You're never alone

> The details are different
> The journey is yours
> But I'm happy to join you
> Holding your doors

Chinks in My Armor

Love is not what I wanted
but what I needed
it's not a rainbow
but a rain bow
angling waterfalls
to cover me
with what I can't escape

I thought I could name it
now I know
to name
is to limit it
is to dismiss it
is to render it
powerless
love is least expected
when it is most needed

try to force it
and it shrinks
try to grab it
and it recoils
try to live it
and it pales
but give up trying
and love
seeps into the cracks
growing flowers
through the chinks in my armor

You Are the One I Come Home To

As people grow old
And feelings get hurt
And minds start to fade
And stutter and spurt
Where do we go to come home to?
Where do we go to come home?

When lives are enmeshed
And then peel away
When tears are all cried
And there's nothing to say
Where do we go to come home to?
Where do we go to come home?

The lessons that are learned
When the dust settles down
And deafening silence
Covers the ground
You are the one I come home to
You are the one that is home

The Heat of My Own Fire

I think I know
why I wanted you to love me
I wanted your love
to fill the hole
that I had carved in my own heart
I wanted your warmth
to burn me alive
to engulf me
to show me who I am
through hot disintegration
I wanted your touch
to desensitize me
And I wanted your breath
to breathe for me
Because I was scared
that if I did it on my own
that no one would like me
that no one would want me
that there wouldn't even be a *me*
to love
You know me now
You know my mind
doesn't plod along
it gallops
it zigs
where it should zag
It falls apart
into the most beautiful mess
I see that now

Because I see *me* now
I see
why I wanted you to love me
I thought
I needed to find love
outside of me

But all along
it waited for me
to stop my endless search
and just sit down
to *the heat of my own fire*
so that I could rest and warm my hands

Love, in Time

love is a crushing
blow to the chest
a gasp
from within
an expelling
of stale air
to breathe in
a renewed sense
of hope
the facade
of perfection
if only
for a moment

does time fade love?
or does love fade time?

Are You Hurt, Son?

Are you hurt, son?
Where have you gone?
The ashes of our last talk
have long stopped smoldering
Are you strong, son?
Only you
can answer that
Just know
when I thought I was
at my strongest
I was
actually
at my weakest

Are you there,
son?

I hear the echoes
of your distant responses
Mere reverberations in my mind
until I find myself again

In Search of Happiness

On a typical day last year
I left in search of happiness
I buttoned my coat and stowed my fear
Expecting a prize for scrappiness

I gasped in surprise
As the road fell away
And I was left with my bundle of fear
So I wrestled it out and opened it up
And my eyes soon started to tear

I hadn't prepared to go it alone
I thought I'd be shown the way
I *wasn't* greeted, I *wasn't* shown
Not a soul appeared to say:
"You won't find the road to happiness here
There's another way you must go
If you follow this path, your route will be clear
And when you've found it, you'll know"

No, no one appeared to help me out
To tell me what I was to do
All I had brought was my fear and my clout
And neither were getting me through

Until I stood up and looked around
To what I hadn't yet seen
Happiness wasn't somewhere to be "found"
It was already inside of me

Hope Is a Funeral

Hope is a battle
A broken dream
A mist, a swamp, a fire
Hope is not what you think it is
It's an uplifting funeral pyre

In Walking, I Find Myself

When I walk
I soar
I lift from the pummeled pavement
When I stroll
I fly
from the gravel down below
I implore you to find
a better way
to sift through thoughts
than a walk once removed
from the drudgery of daily existence
To amble is to wander
down abandoned hallways
wafting words from windswept places
To plod is to punish the past
and cement it in its proper place
I need not the comforts of predictability
nor the empty sounds of mindless chatter
I need a road on which to walk
I need a path to call my home

The Day I Woke Up

The day I woke up
was the day
of my death
the day
I saw
the fragile fall of man
the day
I tasted
the sweet surrender
of who I was
and knew
there was no going back

The day I woke up
was the day
I felt
the cold embrace
of night
of loss
of fear
the day
I knew
it was
it is
all the same
and all the paths
led to
an emergence
out of a punctured dream
And the bursting colors became my life

This Is Not a Poem About Life

this is a poem about life
this is not a poem about death
this is a failure to avoid something
by demanding that it disappear
the harder I push
the more firmly i'm pulled
my creation is its own negation
this is a poem about the process
of sifting, falling, tumbling, crawling
down and through
the learning process we call life
if i take something away
i've created an emptiness
but if I put something back
i've simply transferred space
it's impossible to create a poem about life
because once the words are out
they cease to be accurate
life is the process before the words are released
the moment right before
you and i first met

Ephemeral Disaster

What if your life
is a disaster?
residue from an earthquake
rubble upon rubble
and the sights that you see
a painful reality
are shards
of now-molten glass
from the latest cataclysm
that is your compounding nightmare

But what if your life
is a kaleidoscope?
of ephemeral lights
of hope and despair
of pain and delight
and the sights that you see
they crowd out the blight
to reveal a wondrous thing
It's you, in your life

You Do the Right Thing

doing the right thing
is *not* the easy thing
it's *not* the popular thing
it's the *right thing*
it's the thing you would do regardless
of who is looking
of who is caring
of who *you are*
in relation to
your friends
your family
your life
is a puzzle
as you get older
you figure it out
when you were small
you couldn't even find the pieces
now you have them
but *where* do they go?
where do *you* go
to find yourself?
to steel yourself
against the harsh, acrid winds
of judgment and shame?
you go where you *have* to
you shut up
and learn what you need to
so that when the time comes
you do the right thing

Your Purpose, Revealed

You don't have time.

Your life won't wait.

Moments are passing.

You can't know fate.

Take what you have.

Learn all that you can.

Unleash your heart.

And open your hands.

Swallow your pride.

Engorge humble pie.

Relinquish control.

And blend with the sky.

On the horizon.

Your life is sealed.

Depressing fact?

Or purpose…revealed?

What You Need to Realize

in time you will know
that it wasn't
the searching that got you
where you are
it was the waiting
the feeling
the indomitable presence
that you have
and are

search
and you won't find it
watch
and you won't see it
but plunge
into the murky pool
of existence
and realize
you are already submerged

The Hole That Swallowed You

Do you even remember
the hole that swallowed you?
Or have you
been down there
so long
that even the darkness
feels familiar?
Do you even know
yourself?
And what
you want?
Or are you all dirt
and air?

Below, the roots
that once
grounded you
on which sit
the trees that tower
Above, the soaring sky
way up there
It's limitless
It's effortless
It's free

Why don't you go there?
Because it's cool and
sheltered and
safe
in the hole?

You were born
under the sky
welcomed
by the stars
and held
by the trees,
their branches
forming boughs
that cradled you
branches
connected to roots
searching and reaching
for you
in the hole
that swallowed you
whole

Will My True Life Find Me?

It's a sullen paradise
It's an active dream
A wakefulness soon forgotten
Where nothing's as it seems
I forgot to leave my traces
I went the other way
The people watched me amble
Then went about their days

For no one saw me stalling
Tapping circles with my hands
My knuckles roaring peals
Crossing silence at my command
But the ocean hears me wandering
The hills, they eye my gait
Yet *will* my true life find me?
I better not sit and wait

You Are This Mess. You Are This Life.

How will you know which thread is yours
if you don't pull on a few strands?
The messiness of life
is the tangle of the threads
The tiny rivulets
that will carry you
to your final oceans,
a destination
that can only be spotted
from the center of the mess

You call it tangled

I call it perfectly lost

Open yourself up
to let the mess in
Let it penetrate your heart
with the wisdom
that can only be found
in the path of no escape
How can you escape from something
that cannot be separated
from who *you* are?
You are this mess
You are this life
The knotting and unraveling are one and the same

Claim Your Presence

Are you following
the dream you dreamt
before you were born
the one
that kept your ancestors
up at night?
Are you riding the waves
of the wind that rushes
through the trees
that welcomed you
into this world?
Are you humming the songs
that fluttered in the hearts
of those who loved
you
before you
were born?

Go out
and claim your presence
the one you've known
but still have years to find

Thinking Freely

Ignited by a spark
The mind awakens
And unfurls
To unleash a torrent of thoughts
Overwrought – by what they contain

Unbound and unprovoked
Words are attached
Meanings are construed
To the spontaneous uprising of being

Sensing the need to be controlled
They dodge and dash for safety
Only to emerge, looming large and more imposing

Thoughts, they know no bounds
As they come cascading out
A cerebral flash flood
Rushing to the brink of the fall

Where they plummet
Freely

Hallowed Ground

Will you take me to the hallowed ground, the land of tried and true
Where a myriad of stars stretches near and far
And tether me to you

Will you take me to the hallowed ground, the land of hope and light
Where rocky seas are placid as can be
And rock us to sleep each night

Oh, will you take me to the hallowed ground, the land of fair and fine
Where your body is here, and your heart is near
And your hand is nestled in mind

Doubt

The pangs inside of you
Where once there was truth
Gnaw away and cloud your thoughts

        Like gnats, flitting to and fro
    Exploring the crevices and weaknesses
        Of your weary rumination

Doubt, a soldier in civilian clothing
Mere rubble stronger than any facade

        Doubt, there in the darkness
          Right after the flick
            And flash
        Of a once-lit room

It emerges from spaces yet unsearched
And prowls in caverns yet undiscovered
Waiting
And watching
For a heretofore unknown time

        And it will find you, will it not?

Behind the Pain

Pain is not pain
It's removing the fear
Courage isn't courage
It's removing the pain
Completely different
And one and the same
No matter the path
The outcome remains
Pain is not fear
And fear is not pain

If you told me your answers
I'd have you get more
If you gave me your wisdom
I'd try to ignore
Because deep in my being
is courage and pain
Mixed with some fear
Behind, I remain

When Symptoms Are Behaviors

When symptoms are behaviors
Confusion reigns supreme
In the kingdom of prejudgment
Fear takes hold

A bone is innocuous
A muscle, equally harmless
Blood borders on fear but can be easily managed
But an action, a comment, a stance
That's offensive

Stigma
A word that's often used
But not understood

Because behaviors are symptoms
And people become symptoms, become diagnoses
Become something to box up and ship out
Because packages can be understood
And easily controlled

But healing can't happen in a box
Boxes are for objects
And people aren't objects

When symptoms are behaviors
It's easy to get confused
And box people up
Into a gift that never gets opened

What We See Is Just a Symptom

What we see is just a symptom
Of a deep sickness
Hidden in the core
We look to easy answers
For complex problems
Quick fixes
Not long-term solutions

When a tree won't grow
It would be wise to care for its roots

Hope is empty
Well-wishes could fill entire wells
With the weight of their emptiness
I like kind words
But I like action more
I want compassionate action
Empathetic leadership
More than just hope
More than just wishing well into wells

When randomness reigns
And what we see shocks us
It's easy
To pass it off
As aberration
As something wrong
With the individual
It's harder

To see inside
To what you and I both share
Answers
To intractable problems
But even *more* important
The willingness to take a stand
And make a decision
The desire to begin

Embracing a Single Thought

I remember when I first noticed
The constant thoughts
And the noticing
It was the hardest part

But new awareness
Brought new hope
That somewhere in the thoughts
There was freedom
And a pause
A mere staccato of space to be seized

The mind is tamed when it is noticed
Insight is its own reward
A million-step journey toward the center
Starts by embracing
A single thought

Comparisons

To compare to others
Is a futile act
A circular road
That looks promising
But is banal
And passes familiar sights

A different way to compare
Is to Self-measure
To be your own yardstick
Replenish the water
In your own measuring cup

You always have the time
And the equipment
To run endless experiments
No guesswork needed
Just persistence
And curiosity
Not worrying about what you find
But getting lost in the process
Of comparison
Of learning
About your Self

This is the way to peace
Before you can dance
With another
You must learn to dance
With your Self

So be ruthless in your measurements
All in the pursuit
Of Self-awareness
It is by working on yourself
That you inspire others

I Needed You Yesterday
(But I Didn't Need Anything)

I needed you yesterday
to tell me
today
that tomorrow is here
and I won't lose
my way
that the road I am on
leads back
to my home
but will pass
by strange places
and long
I will roam

                              But I didn't
                              need anything

I had it
with me
I opened
my fear
for the whole world
to see
And the box that contained it
crumpled within
and without, it left me
here, to begin

Mental Health Is

First, mental health is a mimicking of others
Communicating stolen emotion
Showing understanding without self-understanding
A plastering on of papier-mached feelings
The painting of lines in place of natural wrinkles and smiles

Then, mental health is an art project
Painful in its simplicity
Brush strokes of uncertainty
Jagged pencil etchings
Carved too deeply
Because of unknown strength
That is too raw and unfamiliar

Last, mental health is a waking-up
To a bed rocking in a sifting sea of endless waves
But waking up all the same
To the heavy weight and solace of wool blankets
It's a resting place for ceaseless thoughts
A comfort to which one can always return

Love Is

Your love is a precious gift
A glittering gem
A rock warmed by volcanic ash
A diamond hardened by stern knowing and hard reassurance

Your love is like a flower
Wilting under its own weight
But receptive to the cool breeze
That nourishes it
And keeps it afloat
Until ripped from its verdant mooring
By a sudden gushing wind
Alight in its beauty
Soaring higher, breathless
Above the rest, all-knowing and free

But going up is the partner of coming down
Together, they are whole
Natural and connected
Like light and darkness
Hope and despair
Like love and

What is Life

what is life
but a collection of dreams
a reservoir for the soul
a forgotten home
that has ejected
its former residents
into the world
to wreak havoc
as they find their way

what is life
but an open field
pastures burned to create it
fires of footsteps
ravaging new paths
on which tread bodies
far from home
but closer
to where they belong

Ugly Body

Ugly body
Prickly hairs and jagged teeth
Knobby elbows and cracked lips
Connected by skeleton bones and stringy sinews

Toes that go crack
On the cool tile floor
Eyelids that droop
Over filmy lenses

Sandpaper skin, scratching and joining with
Folds of skin that arch
Like rolling waves
That bend and push and stick together
To form an ugly body
With breathtakingly beautiful insides

Caked-On Faces

All of us have a face
that we wear
when we are feeling sad
and crave attention
a face
that we don
when we feel unloved
a public face
a private face
a face that belies
another face we may not even know anymore
Which face is real?
And which is a fabrication?
Or do our collective faces come to shape us?
So that the face we thought we were controlling
becomes the mask that
one day
we forgot to take off
We're all chipping away at caked-on faces
their meanings long forgotten
until
one day
we can't take it anymore
So we remove them all
and the process begins anew

Create the Meaning
of Today

In the footsteps of yesterday
create the meaning of today
Pull the strands of fabric
long forgotten
but able
and wanting
to be mended again
anew
alight
The air is the tapestry
The clouds
ironed hot
on the searing, arcing canvas
Emblazon them on your eyelids
Hold them like you would a friend
you let go of too soon
It's up to you
The meaning's there
The choice is yours

Hope
and it's lost

Act
and it's found

It's the next action

It's the next breath

Discard your inaction
But leave this space
And fill it with meaning

MEANING

On the Eve of Something

We're always on the eve of something
always
about to begin
always building anticipation
for the moment
that will save us
from disappointment
from whatever feeling
we feel
we must escape
But there is no escape
from your life
It's a blast of water
when you expected a trickle
It's clumps of dirt
when you expected fine, iridescent sand

So we create the eve of something
to mold our anticipation
into an ephemeral illusion of control
more beautiful
than the unknowns we love to hate

The Soliloquy of the Soul

The soliloquy of the soul
is a haunting tune
It sings
It moans
and howls for the moon
And all its searching
a hidden boon
wrapped tightly
in the soliloquy of the soul

                    The search for meaning
                    goes far and wide
                    And when you seek it
                    it won't abide
                    because it requires
                    an open mind
                    to listen
                    and wait
                    for the soliloquy of the soul

So if I stand here
and announce my fate
will the Earth bend closer
will harm abate
will *any* other soul
ever relate
to the lessons that are beyond my control
to accompany my begotten soul

The Soil of an Island

when all is the same
who will be the piercing light?
the one who stands
alone
who bends and cuts
when others march?

others feel
the weight
of the world
with bodies, pressed
the burden
is shared, but also
indistinguishable

I choose to be free
with my thoughts
with my dreams
with the way
I see the world

I watch them all
float by
on a sea
of sameness
they live
for the waves
the rolling weekends
I am an island
long gone from Pangaea
who still feels
the homeland in his soil

Do You See What I See?

Are you free?
Are you on the wings of the dream?
Do you believe in the future?
Do you see what I see?

Earth is slipping so softly
the rug from your feet
the hope from your eyelids
the sword from your sheath
It's a crescendo of footsteps
It's a staccato of beats
The old dream is dawning
Do you see what I see?

Empty Space

What *happens* with words unsaid
That create the empty space?
Where do we go, how do we tread
When free from keeping pace?

> What *happens* to silent faces
> When words don't crowd the air?
> Silent eyes dancing silent traces
> When no one is "right" or "fair?"

What *happens* to broken dreams
When silence fills the place?
Do they disappear into open seams
Or grow to fill the space?

What If Today

what if today
were the last time
you wake up
and see the sun
feel the wind
hear the leaves
falling
to the ground
did you forget to hear them?
did you miss the feeling of the wind
biting through your bones?
did the sun escape your glance?

what if today
were the last time
you heard the voice
of the one
who you profess to love
and who
loves you?
would it be
the most melodic sound
you've ever heard?
or
would it be
grating
like cheese, not chalk
pushed through
falling down

changing shape
a menial task
the marvels of which
such simple slicing
are all but forgotten

in days among days
all but forgotten
would you notice it?

if not tomorrow,
what if today?

Maps Are Liars

I thought I would find what I was looking for
In plans and maps of my dreams
But it wasn't there
It wasn't life
It wasn't what it seemed

        I thought I could muscle my future
        Into the broad, idyllic light
        But fate had other plans for me
        It had designed another life

Soon I realized the fallacy
Of wishing for paths to be mine
I had to learn to trust myself
And open up my eyes

        Maps are liars
        They create false visions
        Of where I thought I would go
        Now I know I'll see much more
        If I relax and join the flow

Distant Spaces

Distance creates in the mind
a fondness for closeness
for knowing what is important
and what is most meaningful
If you take the time
to separate yourself
from yourself
you will see what I mean

Create the space
and you will find
the gaps in the clutter
Open your heart
and you will feel
the space between the beating
The flutter of thoughts
escape from the crevices of mental caverns
The soft sinews of stolen moments
are waiting
So take the time to find them

Here is your task
Escape that which you're immersed in
Plunder your long-lost memories
to find the passions of your youth
those lonely obsessions
that you alone could feel
in a distant time
in a solitary place
Go back
and find yourself
in the distant spaces you once knew so well

The Ever Afterglow

Life is a rocky landscape
It's a battlefield shorn by love
It's a pockmarked desert
It's caverns of hope
It's the skies raining down from above

Life, it's luminous, if you let it
And if you don't
Dark swallows you whole
You must uplift your life
You must seize it
You must grab by the horns then let go

For your life, you must illuminate it
Center stage and ready to go
The curtain is rising—and now there you are
In life, the ever afterglow

The Purpose of Fear

fear, pervasive fear
great weaver of our woes
you stop the heart
blacken the treads
and clench us amidst your throes
you hold us back
but we need you
you tell us we can't
when we must
because it's precisely by disobeying you
that in ourselves we learn to trust
fear, pervasive fear
sapper of strength and fight
if our resolve could be any stronger
it's because you've created our plight
for fear is the path of the warrior
of the timid and arrogant, too

        fear shapes the destinies of all of us
        our lessons not away, but through

Ask Me a Question

They say the best answers
come from the greatest questions
But who are *they*?
And why do they say that?
I say,
I trust what I know
I see the answers in my own questions
I feel my senses plucking strings in the universe
sending the vibrations down my spine
connecting me back to the reverberating source
the pool from which my questions emerge
If I asked you a question
would you know the answer?
You'd know what you know but
how would you find out more?
Through questions
thought beacons
searching for the answers
through murky depths
and scintillating skylines
They are all the same
A mere backdrop for the dance
of question and answer
call and response
of to and fro
Ask me a question
And hear the roar of my "I don't know"

The Answer to Your Life Is
in the Details

The answer to your life
is in the details
in the flowers
of your mind
the ones
you forgot to water
whose seeds
you forgot to plant
birthed from the decisions
you forgot to make

Open your soul window
Air out your feelings
but don't try
too hard

Ease into
the moment
Slip into
the substance of life
The ripples on the surface
let you know

You're alive

Where I Trace My Lines

why did it take so long
to be myself
to open my arms
to embrace
who I am?
the miles I have walked
in others' shoes
in clothes unknown
reading yesterday's news

today is the day
I find myself
I throw open the windows
to the fresh air
that I left behind in my youth
to the open spaces
from which I emerged
through which I will pass
and to which I will go
it was always
supposed to be this way

ending up
on a road, willfully predetermined
these empty spaces are
where I trace my lines

It's What's Beneath That Matters Most

You don't see the struggle behind these walls
You don't hear the rushing blood or feel the stringy sinews
You don't see the space within, closed off from the world
Or smell the sweating madness, dripping with passion
I've heard others have this, too
Their own private battles
Behind their own armored walls
That they wage hidden wars
Much like I fight my own
The world is a harsh canvas
Aggressive brushstrokes across a page
Arcs already chosen
Colors predetermined
So much paint caked on
That it takes years for it to flake off
And reveal what's underneath
You may comment on my colors
Admire the highlights in my tapestry
Inside this portrait that we share
The one on which I know — and you know — the flaking off
Of paint chips
The fleeing of prismatic flecks
Is not a flaw in the design
It's a revealing
An unleashing
Of what was there all along
Telling you
It's what's beneath that matters most

So That Others Can Find Your Current

If you could see
the potential you have
If you could feel
the mountain you'd move
If only you knew
that your greatest moment
is around the bend
That the curve in the road
is *not* a setback
but the moment
that you look
to the exact spot
where your *meaning* is forged
where your beliefs are changed
where the world
sees you
for who you are

I don't doubt you
What holds you back
is the impasse
you have built in your own mind
the moat upon which
you will construct your boat
So that others can find your current
and follow you

A Song for the Suffering

This is a song for the suffering
for the ones who have lost their way
the ones who can't find their direction
can't find the words they know they must say

> This is a song for the aimless
> the ones whose paths have grown dim
> for you, for me
> for our sisters and brothers
> our weary hearts and all our worn limbs

Your road is not predetermined
your feelings, not set in stone
And although it feels that nothing will change
change is the one constant we know

> Did you know that all leaders have suffered?
> Did you know why they're fit to lead?
> It's because they got lost that they found their way
> It's because you are blind that you see

This is a song for the suffering
for you who reads these notes
And it's the mere fact you've made it this far
that proves you have much farther to go

Becoming Who You Are

When did it start?
the process
of becoming who you are?
When did you know?
what you
were meant to be?
How did you find?
the stars
that you alone could see?
Why did you turn?
down that *one road*
and not the other?

Life is a carpet
unfurling
becoming flat
and sturdy
with every passing step
You are pressing down
crystallizing the path
that is becoming
who
you
are

About the Author

Jordan Brown is a mental health advocate, writer, and entrepreneur. He's been blogging and tweeting to make mental health more accessible and meaningful since 2016. Formally trained as a social worker, Jordan considers his mental health struggles and open-heart surgery the greatest, most life-affirming lessons of all. You can connect with him on Twitter (@jpbrown5) or through his weekly mental health email newsletter, *The Mental Health Update*, at newsletter.thementalhealthupdate.com. He is tolerated by his lovely wife and cats in Missoula, Montana.

Made in the USA
Columbia, SC
22 September 2020